MEETING THE TORMENTORS
IN SAFEWAY

MEETING THE TORMENTORS in SAFEWAY

ALEXANDRA OLIVER

BIBLIOASIS
Windsor, Ontario

FIRST EDITION

Library and Archives Canada Cataloguing in Publication

Oliver, Alexandra, 1970-
      Meeting the tormentors in safeway / Alexandra Oliver.

Issued also in electronic format.
ISBN 978-1-927428-43-6

      I. Title.

PS8629.L54M44 2013   C811'.6   C2013-902000-4

Biblioasis acknowledges the ongoing financial support of the Government of Canada through the Canada Council for the Arts, Canadian Heritage, the Canada Book Fund; and the Government of Ontario through the Ontario Arts Council.

Readied for the press by Zachariah Wells
Copy-edited by Tara Murphy
Typeset and designed by Kate Hargreaves
PRINTED AND BOUND IN CANADA

CONTENTS

[Medium-long shot: at a food depot, a woman stands over a fallen policeman, her arms full of loot.]

NARRATOR:

This is Mrs. Joyce Fisher from Gravesend. She was a housewife. Three yards from her, the bodies of the military guard. When morale falls, ideals fall and may go, and behaviour becomes more primitive, more a thing of instinct.

—*Original screenplay, Peter Watkins'* The War Game

THE PROMISE WE MADE
TO THE EARTHQUAKE

I'm going to turn my back on death, forsaking
fatalistic anomie. I'll forge
a human heart from rogue tectonic plates,
a way to make the flocks of birds return.
I'll wait until the church has ceased to burn,
the arms to pull away from iron gates,
rebel against geology in rage.
I swear I'll do it when my hands stop shaking.

I'm going to turn the world back by a day,
raise stone walls and conjure panes of glass
from mournful piles of sand and broken streets.
I'll tell my neighbour what he means to me,
give back his toaster, skis, and new TV.
I'll make the rude wind raise tarpaulin sheets
and let them part until the children pass
to parents resurrected from the clay.

I'm turning over fifty-two new leaves.
I'm going to speak with kindness to my wife
and tell my baser thoughts to disappear.
I will not steal my brother's medications,
fake illness at my in-laws' celebrations,
or make my office intern weep in fear.
I fell apart so I could make my life
a binding deal within a den of thieves.

I swear to you that, when the ground stops shaking,
I'll put this day behind me like a dream.
I'll step out with my ordinary hands,
clear lumber and lay bricks for twenty years,

re-irrigate the gardens with my tears,
endeavour to be one who understands
how our own better angels can redeem
a country from the hell of earth's own making.

CHINESE FOOD WITH GAVRA, AGED THREE

We choose a corner table, far away
from jars of chopsticks, tempting potted trees.
The wine list? No. *The lunchtime special?* Please.
You thrill to this diversion in your day,
the clack of plastic spoons, the smooth ballet
of plates and bowls passed out in Cantonese
and then, you're craning forward on your knees,
and rocking in your chair. *Mum look!* You say.

Our placemats swirl with dragons, dogs, and rats,
an explanation of the beasts within
each one of us, born under some mute star
of venom, talons, teeth. Please tell me that's
the other ones, my joyful mandarin,
you, crowing like the rooster that you are.

OTTAWA WALK-IN CLINIC
WAITING ROOM, 9PM

The girl at the desk lives in fear of the phone.
The boy in the chair keeps his foot on a plant.
An old lady mouths her novenas, alone;
I read our phone number out like a chant.

The college kid barks in the crook of his arm.
The bum takes his sock off to check the infection.
A poster describes the contagion and harm
of love under bridges without one's protection.

While cold-hearted bulbs keep an eye on the gloom,
our son will not take his prescription of fear
but joyfully buzzes in loops round the room
because he's been told there's a bug in his ear.

PRESCHOOL

Tim predicts the weather on a hunch.
Olivia's seen *Triumph of the Will*.
Norris, after church and Sunday brunch,
picks up the bill.

Nicky uses words like "gaunt" and "strung."
Philomena naps with jars of bees.
Terence vanishes—we find he's hung
his toys in trees.

Annabelle writes *pesticide*, by choice.
Carter's learned to waken in a sweat.
Paula tells us, in a quiet voice,
"I'm not done yet."

PARTY MUSIC

Friends, applaud. The comedy is over.
—*Ludwig van Beethoven*

In '68 a great conductor came
to one small European town. His flat
was right above our Gran's. He reeked of fame,

wore grey ostrich shoes, a beaver hat
tipped on a sweep of hair now going white,
a coat in astrakhan. A man like that

deserved the name of *meister.* Appetite
for drama and excitement won at last;
we wondered what he did, by day and night,

the aura of an enigmatic past
(unknown to us, small girls of six and eight)
now flattened by the neutral atom blast

of Swissness. We could only speculate;
he was a mighty river with no source.
But we had watched him leave the building late:

a sleigh pulled by a giant yellow horse
had scooped him up, a Russian at his side.
An undernourished blonde in mink. Of course.

What more could any human being provide?
We had it figured out. We knew this man
was perfect for a widow, bona fide

salvation for the suffering of Gran,
whose patience was as solid as the stones
on Via Maestra. So we made a plan,

imagined, in soft, out-of-focus tones,
her breathless lurking near the fire stairs.
Notified (a buzz between two phones),

down he'd slink to orchestrate affairs;
although our minds had not digested sex,
we grimly guessed what adults did in pairs.

He'd ring the bell, come in for tea. The next
instalment of our hot imaginings:
her jewelled hands upon his goat-haired pecs,

(insert a full accompaniment of strings)
as preface to the cinematic kiss,
his man-purse chucked aside! Like mighty wings

those sideburns swooped on in. Oh, great abyss
she toppled into, blown by some gust
of sweet, forbidden philharmonic bliss.

All this for romance in the upper crust,
a man above domestic life's dull take,
a Mercury, to whom we pinned in trust

the soft and sparkling trappings of a rake,
all caviar and aftershave, the gold
of damask curtains, opened by mistake.

Party member, that phrase of cold
and adult truth was just one part left out
of what the two of us were later told.

It wasn't what we'd hoped to think about,
for party used to mean the happy mess,
the donkey tail, the streamers and the shout,

the ripple of a silver satin dress,
a belch of pink confetti in the air,
but now we heard the coda of distress:

the rattle of a door against a chair,
the flutter of the bitter yellow stars
that, long ago, three cousins had to wear.

No nothing, whether sequin, crumb or shred,
no fur, no silk, no balcony guitars,
the strains of the *Horst Wessel Lied* instead.

Because, of course, the Party wasn't ours.

RIMSKY-KORSAKOV
ON FIFTH AVENUE

Today there's a boy in the bookshop café
In frock coat and black satin vest
And a hat and a cane and a silver pince-nez
And a pocket watch tucked in his breast.

He tells me he's Russian and likes to compose
(Folk opera's big in demand),
And he somehow seems more than a loon in old clothes,
So I reach for his thin, offered hand.

I wonder what colours the life that he leads;
(How often are people unkind?
Does some other age give all that he needs?)
I follow him now, in my mind:

I picture him later, on one of the trains—
The passengers goggle with groans,
Make fingertip squiggles right next to their brains,
Nudge neighbours, take pictures with phones.

His family waits by the small garden wall
On the coldest of cold Jersey nights,
And nothing is Russian here, nothing at all,
But he is the brightest of lights.

Though not quite what Bubba describes as a *mensch,*
Such love is a fixed guarantee,
As they listen for scrapes of the Schweighofer's bench
And wait for the flight of the bee.

THE VILLAGE ARSONIST
KUMBOR, MONTENEGRO

A match. That's all a person needs to do it
when others lie unconscious in their beds.
Original is the best label out there;
I see its letters burn in golds and reds.

The women step into the road, encumbered
with washing and the flat, black weight of years,
deciding daily, somehow, *should I die here*
I'd like my ghost to be that thing he fears.

By "he" they mean their men, who haven't wakened
in ages. Here they come now, barrelling,
raging, *Arson bastard! Someone stop him!*
Mighty like sparks that make the tinder sing.

You see, I'm old, I fought the Germans, hanging
on hope, the party, and on the ripe blast
of flame, but who will think this world needs changing?
Fires of that world, they flare in the dead past,

leaving the soft, grey, unilluminated
nowhere of now, where cruise ships churn
—those islands made of smoke, flags, and iron—
wretchedly cold. Oh, as a plain gold urn

I hold the best of all that sits here burning—
for I can make every betrayed rose burn.

THE WIDOWS
ĐJENOVIĆI, MONTENEGRO

We, who regard the undertow
we swim in, when black clouds creep,
have learned no fear; death lives in us,
ripening wealth, like green vines asleep.

Treading the quiet dust,
miracles fade—our young are going.
We broach the sea to find our own:
a god in a boat of silver, rowing.

A CHILD'S CHRISTMAS IN THE SOCIALIST FEDERAL REPUBLIC OF YUGOSLAVIA
(For D.B.)

When I was little, we had Christmastime,
like you, but with a Socialistic bent.
We had stockings, gifts, a clinking tree
and, best of all, we had our Santa Claus
whom we called Deda Mraz, or Grandpa Frost.
We thought of him, and all sang-froid was lost;
when he came in the party hall, applause
would thunder from the palms of ninety-three
small children, whose glum parents had all spent
hours gearing up to brave the pantomime.

They dressed us in our best, our neckerchiefs
like little scarlet birds that swirled the room
colliding with each other. Giant bows
grew out of female hair, and pleated pants,
though polyester, dignified the boys.
We craned our necks to see the bag of toys.
Our mothers were the Fox Fur Commandants:
God help you if you tried to pick your nose
or one would rise, a nimbus of perfume
that heralded the smacks, the yowls, the sniffs.

Deda Mraz would ask each kid to say
if he or she had been good all year round.
Then, tuning out replies about the spats
and peeing in one's pants at Pioneers,
the paper glue in someone's teacher's shoes
(resulting in a most impressive bruise),
would rummage for a toy. To feral cheers,
he'd follow up with sweets and paper hats,

and special tangerines produced around
the place where Tito took his holiday.

Someone in my school relayed the facts,
that Deda Mrazes weren't the same old guy
but differed every year. Their beards were real,
long and dirty, reservoirs of stuff
that old men had about. But they were all
ex-Partizans. In seven-year-old thrall,
I found this information quite enough
to keep afloat the Christmas man's appeal.
I saw him in my mind, against a sky
of blood, resisting Germans with an axe.

And then I saw November, all the men
and women from The Party Room. They'd burst
into some tenement, a tenuous match
to some description. Fighting off the pong
of onions and mazout, with clipboards, rope
and cameras they come, engorged with hope.
They find some poor old guy to drag along
(one hand inside his underpants, mid-scratch)
and shove him in a Zastava, head first,
to start the churning cycle up again.

I was inches taller than my peers
and, when I shuffled forward for my loot
with pleated trousers grieving for more hem
and head that bumped the swooping tinsel stars,
I felt the eyes of all those furry mums
(amongst the candies, Sindy dolls, and drums,
and sickly whirr of plastic Chinese cars)
who tagged my coltish wonder as a sham,
questioned why I needed toys and fruit
with such a blatant overheap of years.

And then the shit would hit the Christmas Fan:
some teacher lurking cruelly in the back
would point in my direction, cough and say,
I think our little Dragan wants to tell
you, Deda Mraz, about how very glad
we are to have you here. And if I'd had
a spade, I would have dug a hole to hell
and jumped, but no, this was the wretched day
the biggest boy was summoned from the pack
to celebrate the state's most festive man.

And so I did it. Sniggering and grins
ignored, I ventured to the peeling throne.
I peered into the brandy-bleary stare
and burbled out the fragments of a speech
that scattered like a country blown apart.
Where is he now, that valiant old fart?
Time puts ones like him well out of reach,
but how much sweetness we had hidden there
in tinsel, cake and socialistic stone—
and, most of all, in Tito's mandarins.

CURRICULUM VITAE

I may be wrong, but I'm never in doubt.
—*Marshall McLuhan*

In '75, I drew the letter 'n'
backwards, stapled Allison's left hand,
smoked Dad's last Montecristo, tore pell-mell
through aisles on flights abroad (no matter where),
yelled "poo!" in church, propelled a bag of bread
at someone's mother, piddled in the bed,
took a whack at cutting my own hair,
and ran away from Mum in some hotel
in Mexico. If dragged upon the stand,
I'd pledge myself to do it all again.

In 1986, I went to meet
a boy who liked to carry a grenade,
crawled out the window to go and see the Cramps
while under curfew, peeled my own split ends,
set fire to Comet, lost my mother's ring,
complained when she was calm enough to sing,
wreaked havoc on my most enduring friends,
and broke a pair of ugly crystal lamps
in Hudson's Bay. If I could be remade,
I'd hit the switch that said, in red, REPEAT.

In '98, I drove a man to tears,
drank all night and jumped the subway stile,
not once, but twice. I snubbed the homeless, swore,
made eager interviewees ill-at-ease,
fought my secretary, spent paycheques
on underwear and hash for sloppy sex.
The hive of hell was crowded with my bees,
the sea of ill acquainted with my oar

but, asked if I would overwrite my file,
I'd walk away with cotton in my ears.

And now's the time to cast the vipers out,
sow sweetness, stagger on towards the light,
be loyal, leave behind the louche romances,
scale down the height of all my shoes,
lash my weary person to the mast,
and aim for heaven. *This is how you last,*
they tell me, *cut the sparking fuse;*
a woman doesn't get too many chances.
I wonder if respectable means right;
I'm waiting to be rescued by my doubt.

SEXUAL HISTORY

Under my window they stood, with their hands
waving tickets to *Carmen* and keys to the Porsche.
They had cups full of sugar and cables to start
up the car in the parking lot, matches and pens
and the right time of day, on the path in the park.
They were gentle with animals, children and plants,
and used words like *forever* and *always* and *now*.
When they vanished, their feet walked away with no sound.
In the past, in the dark, under wraps, underground,
oh, the men before you. They were tow-haired and tall.

Oh, the men before you. They were square and morose.
They had bat wings for souls and racks of grey teeth,
and a family somewhere that I'd never meet.
They had hundreds of poker chips stacked by the bed
and, instead of declaring their love made them weak,
they would give me commands through their suffering phones,
using words like *don't know*, and *unsure* and *not now*.
Hanging up, leaving only the feeling of down.
Oh, they did me a favour, the men before you,
as they dug themselves deep, in the past, underground.

THE CLASSICS LESSON

I told him about Galatea,
the joyful, animated queen.
He told me, *make it short—I have
three discs of porn I haven't seen.*

I told him she was fashioned by
Pygmalion's skilled and lonely hand.
He told me, *that's the kind of thing
a guy could never understand.*

I told him that he whispered pleas
and vows into her chilly ear.
He answered, *where's the damn remote,
and who forgot to buy the beer?*

I told him that he brought her shells
and little birds and shining stones.
He told me, *get a pad and pen.
I'll need them if my agent phones.*

I told him that he laid her out
in purple on a gilded chaise.
He told me, *I'll be working late
tonight, and for the next five days.*

I told him that he went to pray
for someone like his sculpted one.
He said, *the baby wrecked your boobs;
If I were you, I'd get them done.*

I told him that he hurried home
and pressed her to his pounding heart.
He said, *the therapist was right,*
that we could use some time apart.

I told him that she came to life
and both lived loving evermore.
He told me, *damn, I'm out of smokes.*
I'll go and get some at the store.

He told me, *I forgot my keys.*
He told me, *hey, it's ten below.*
He told me, *open this damn door.*
I told him no. I told him no.

TEST CAPE

I've landed on a way to try you out
and gauge your mettle. Please put on this cape.
(It's far too late to think about escape).
I'd like you now to venture out without

your other clothes. The cape will have to do.
Go down to Omar's Maxi Milk and buy
a pack of Belmont Milds, and would you try
to see if they have raisin bread? Milk too.

When you reach across to get the change,
contrive a little conversation. Muse
about the way the Raiders always lose.
Say thank you. Take your time and rearrange

your stuff inside the bag. And please try not
to panic. You'll need Herculean force
to pull it off. You are aware, of course,
it's August, and it's criminally hot,

and Omar has that huge electric fan
he borrowed from the film set just last week.
If you are not arrested as a freak,
I'll know you are no ordinary man.

TEMPLATE FOR A CONVERSATION
WITH A SINGLE FRIEND

I'll call you back when Junior is in bed
(addressed to Isa/Janet/Winifred).
My hands are full of turkey parts and string;
I know you want to talk about the thing
that happened at the staff retreat with Ted.

I have to see the kids are bathed and fed.
Of course I'd rather talk to you instead.
I'm sure he doesn't view it as a fling—
I'll call you back.

I'm sure he only means to clear his head.
You can't expect a man to go to bed
with someone from the office and then ring.
You have a lot to give. Stop hollering,
stop saying that you wish that you were dead.
I'll call you back.

ONE OF THESE DAYS

It's Monday in the soggy park. We clump
barnacular against the little wall.
That thing's a loneliness, that blackened hump
we try to climb. The hours are all

so tightly knitted: waking, messy meals,
the robust smell of diaper and the squirms
of legs resisting stroller straps. It feels
profane to covet friendship on those terms.

The sweatsuits shuffle, hands scratch digits down
on cards and old receipts. What lost soul calls
to talk about the pram, the birthday clown,
the infant gyms in vast suburban malls?
I stop, assume my focused-mother glaze.
When will you call?
                    Oh, soon—one of these days.

VOTED BEST PLACE TO LIVE

The bend of the lake is deceptively perfect;
its water shines silver in punishing sunlight
as seen from the pier, where the park was constructed.
Now, calm and unruffled, its threat is the greatest:
it promises shelter to all that it swallows.

See how the sun travels up, travels down,
throws petals of gold in the hair of the parents,
their hopes climbing high as they wait at the gates
that split themselves open at three on the dot,
spilling the children in red tartan uniforms.

A town full of children is anyone's garden.
They tended me till I could take it no more.
I knew I would bloom when I looked at the lake,
the flatness of rubber, the odour of tar—
united, they whispered, *it's fine under here.*

I left a short note with my shoes at the railing.
No one had pegged me as that kind of person,
as I was in second-year law at McMaster,
liked to run marathons, played the piano,
and never gave anyone cause for alarm.

My mother and father grew prize-winning roses,
copied by no one; a beauty so terrible,
rumoured to rival the best in Ontario,
quietly, quietly growing and dying
and always remembered in ribbons and silver.

MEETING THE TORMENTORS
IN SAFEWAY

They all had names like Jennifer or Lynne
or Katherine; they all had bone-blonde hair,
that wet, flat cut with bangs. They pulled your chair
from underneath you, shoved their small fists in
your face. Too soon, you knew it would begin,
those minkish teeth like shrapnel in the air,
the Bacchic taunts, the Herculean dare,
their soccer cleats against your porcine shin,
that laugh, which sounded like a hundred birds
escaping from a gunshot through the reeds—
and now you have to face it all again:
the joyful freckled faces lost for words
in supermarkets, as those red hands squeeze
your own. *It's been so long!* They say. Amen.

DOUG HILL

I want the sun to swallow up Doug Hill,
said the tenth-grade student (through her tears).
He said he loved me, but he never will;
I can't go on like this for sixty years.

Said the tenth-grade student, through her tears,
he said he needed time and he would call.
I can't go on like this for sixty years.
I can't go on. I can't go on at all.

He said he needed time and he would call.
He brushed the leaves from off his pants and rose.
I can't go on. I can't go on at all,
I thought, and reached in darkness for my clothes.

He brushed the leaves from off his pants and rose
the next day. Back at school, they looked at me,
I thought. I reached in darkness for my clothes,
feeling bare and horrible and free.

The next day, back at school. They looked at me,
but all I saw was him, though he was gone,
feeling bare and horrible and free.
I am the one the tigers fell upon.

And all I see is him, though he is gone.
I see him in the locker doors, the sky.
I am the one the tigers fell upon.
I want the bell to ring. I want to die.

I see him in the locker doors, the sky;
he said he loved me, but he never will.
I want the bell to ring. I want to die.
I want the sun to swallow up Doug Hill.

THE GIRLS AND THE EELS

Now, trawling round the high streets, I can see
this weird, black, glittered wave, the girls borne high
on surfboards unseen to the naked eye,
their soft shell bellies peeping teasingly
and colt legs crammed in boot-tops. Click, the heels
wade into the undiscovered sea,
all shipwrecks and the tender teeth of eels.

What is there beneath the glittered wave,
between the rocks and weeds that stream like hair?
Could anything their mothers said prepare
them for this airless thrill, the grave?
Their mothers dropped the diving bell beneath.
They told them there were many fish down there;
they led them to the wreckage and the teeth.

THE GULLS

The gulls come down to oversee the lake;
their wings splay out like halves of open books.
The beach is filling up and, by the looks
of things, we've made a vague mistake.
There's little room for us to spread our towels
among the penguin men, the girls with rooks'
eyes all alert, the timid matron owls.

My smiling, pale son goes off to play.
A truck is parked beside the ice cream shack
and, from a falcon's wing, big knuckles crack
against a woman's jaw. I hear him say,
You keep your smart mouth shut. I take the fries,
try not to watch the bruised flight of her back.
The gulls beg off now, swallowed in soft cries.

USING THE PUBLIC BINOCULARS
AT SHERBET LAKE DISCOVERY CENTRE

They're gentrifying Sherbet Lake.
They've built a Centre on the slopes
near waters which stretch out for miles
and weakly beat the promenade.
Despite the modern glass façade
and cheery bleached ceramic tiles,
despite the mayor's greatest hopes,
perhaps the effort was half-baked.

They're chipping into Sherbet Lake.
They'll carve a diamond from the rock
of land that once belonged to farms
and scatter it with bright boutiques.
The Centre opens in four weeks;
a giant billboard shouts its charms:
A viewing deck! A spa! A dock,
a dry martini, charbroiled steak.

But, from the deck at Sherbet Lake
I see no bistros, no vitrines.
The big box stores squat blankly by
the sad and gusting freeway mouth.
The factories are headed south.
All best-laid plans have gone awry;
they leave behind the pregnant teens,
the poor, the unspecific ache.

I turn my back on Sherbet Lake,
the blinders of this perfect park;
I see the ills with my own eyes
for fifty cents. The silent mills

discovered by the ochre hills,
ignored, diminishing in size.
Bring on the creeping autumn dark.
The lights:

        what difference will they make?

ESCAPING THE ICE

The sports club, circa 1974,
had orange halls with trophies, snaps and flags;
our parents liked the modernist décor
inside the lounge (where they could smoke their fags).

They sat and gossiped while, beyond the glass,
way down below, we toddled on our blades
and huffed through every forty-minute class.
That's me: the snowsuit with the fussy braids.

The child in that photo over there
is Anna; she already had thirteen
official badges, plus the lion's share
of local trophies. All of us were keen

to stay and watch her cut the numbers in
the glassy surface, loved to hear the tape
go click, until *Bolero* would begin.
She had a crimson skirt and little cape

she wore for that routine. She lived for show
in shadow. With her mother, leaning close
against the window, in the amber glow,
ambition meted out in overdose,

white-knuckled at the charlotte and the lutz,
muttering *sotto voce*, as the checks
and camel spins of lamb-chop skirted butts
obscured her line of vision from the decks,

before she scuttled down and seized the arm
that glorified the butterfly and swan
and, in a Slavic blast of hot alarm,
re-froze the surface that we stood upon.

The years went by. We put our skates aside,
went in for tennis, softball and ballet,
learned how to draw a bow and how to ride.
Don't ask us how to do those things today.

Did Anna also manage to unlearn
the attitudes, the spirals and the checks,
allow herself the satisfying burn
of imperfection, self-indulgence, sex?

We only know she went and disappeared
in '82, without a final bow,
but just a note (my cousin volunteered
the news): *Dear Mom, my program's over now.*

Thinking of that medal load in crates,
I'm glad that Anna made a Russian split
and bolted like a rabbit for the gates.
Most brave the cold and make the best of it.

MRS. MILLER LAYS IT OUT TO HER DAUGHTER AT THE AUDITION, MARCH 23, 1985

Know that your beauty is all that you have—
a luminous, numinous guide to the dark,
to a world where the windows are fogged with desire—
a flash of the dagger, an interesting spark.

Nothing can stop what is smooth or burns bright.
Unhindered by fat or by bone or by rash,
it soars like a satellite over the heads
of women whose bloom has dissolved into ash.

And what of the book and the life of the mind
and hair that hangs loose by the cup and the lamp
and the scratch of a pen? That is for men.
And you, my slim cygnet, are not of that camp.

The other girls wait with their freckles and hands
full of flowers and notes. Their voices are real
but their friendship is not. They will use you for blood.
They will crumple you under their terrible wheel.

Hold on to your weapons, the spike and the tooth.
Go out there and slay them. The day will come soon
when you stand on the roof and it dawns on you there:
You are nothing, outshone by the unageing sun.

FIXING THE OLD FOLKS' HOME

A month ago, some builders buckled down
to tear the balconies from the face
of a large tower in this part of town
about a hundred metres from our place.
From where I sit, I see the sliding doors
of each compartment glisten through the dust,
which sifts up, golden, as the great drill roars.
Does this display disturb the calm? It must,
it's one more rattled building site, but no,
it makes a moment: workers swarm and pass.
The barriers torn down, the air says, go!
while residents behind the mumbling glass
imagine stepping out boldly, to forsake
Newton, and soar like moths above the lake.

HOW ARE YOU, BUNNY?

And Bunny's standing in the laundry room,
her mottled knuckles round a jug of Cheer.
(A year ago, it would have been Ron here,
but now the park below is in full bloom
and Ron is gone. They took away his chair,
his IV stand, his magazines, his stains,
the view he loved: his lake and rusting cranes.
None of this, of course, is my affair.)
The sorted load I toss to chase my words,
but none will do. No sentiments outclean
the leading brand, that bastard Mr. Death.
Outside, the wires throng with grimy birds.
I hear it as she shuts the last machine—
I'm fine—to no-one, on her change-cold breath.

TAKING CARE

Realize one day they will be gone
and make sure they have everything they need.
See always that a light has been left on.

Plump the cushions in the grey salon,
keep the doctor's office up to speed.
Realize one day they will be gone.

The tea, the pills, their orange juice and scone,
their tray, the folded *Post* for them to read.
See always that a light has been left on.

But who decided children should be strong
and need for nurture sublimated greed,
their parents' warm authority half-gone?

What turned your father into Genghis Khan,
your mum into Tisiphone in tweed?
See always that a light has been left on—

one day, the darkness will descend upon
your head. Though neighbours tell you you've been freed
(*of course, you knew one day they would be gone*),
see always that a light remains left on.

WHAT YOU WANT THE DOCTOR
TO TELL YOU
(For Herbert Arnold Dimitri Oliver, 1921-2011)

There was nothing we could ever do
to keep him in the world. He just escaped.
His brain said, "Hold that thought!" and there he went—
left the intern feeling like a dunce.
His five bad habits failed him, all at once;
we lost his bile and all embarrassment
from monitors; the spiked, green line re-scaped
into a placid sea, and then we knew.

His gut was pierced with arrows of surprise.
A great idea burst inside his mind
and, as it did, his lungs ballooned with song.
We tried to move on in. Our hands were tied;
we checked the ultrasound and saw, inside
his bloodstream, a small boat that chugged along
towards his heart, to take him to the kind
place where he could see the red sun rise.

OVER A FABERGÉ OWL

A bright-eyed but humourless thing
stands vigil, as the day grows dark,
its plume a shield, cold as a shield.
Its gaze ignores the view, the park.

Fussed over for its wild worth,
itemized in estimates and wills,
it disregards all human ills,
while the inheritors of Earth

(unmarbled, with no Tsarist sheens),
outside, as roughened moonlight blanches,
wait: wrath keen in the evergreens,
claws calmly gripping those live branches.

THE TOY CATALOGUE
OF THE AFTERLIFE

Plane that takes rejection to the moon
Table soccer set that comes with cheers
Clay that shapes a Sunday afternoon
Science kit that runs on bread and tears

Whistle (when you blow it, falcons come)
Sword designed to rise from silver lakes
Grand piano smaller than a thumb
Baking set for pearl and diamond cakes

Slinky made from lovers' DNA
Magnet letters for the anguished tongue
Robot spouting Crane and Mallarmé
Superhero cape that keeps you young

Kite that gets away in calmest weather
Talking bear that tells you *come back soon*
Lego blocks that put the soul together
Drum that bangs the first-remembered tune

THE GHOSTS OF THE SPACE DOGS

Everyone is their friend in cosmic darkness:
sweeping under the capsule, miles of oceans,
dancing trees full of little mottled birds, and
somewhere there is a meadow, huge and windy.

Waiting there are the patient, smiling People,
white coats billowing, waving giant sticks and
shouting, *Honeybee! Foxy! Laika! Get it!*
That is, maybe, what all those Space Dogs thought of.

We who lie under starlight know they're up there,
circling: science's cheerful lost explorers,
suited, pressurized, bully beef and biscuits
ready; now, with the booster rockets silent.

Not the dizzying swell of rising heat and
not the carbon dioxide building slowly,
filling dog brains with thoughts of clouds and rabbits,
words of gentle murmurings, belly-scratching fingers;

not the creeping parades with jeeps and banners,
farm girls stirring the air with hoes and rifles,
nor the rapturous sighs of stamp collectors,
pausing thoughtfully over Laika's image,

placed with tweezers on mats of tufted velvet,
green, unfurled, like the best of all intentions,
like an arm with a stick cast forth to orbit,
like a meadow flush with celestial rabbits.

Watching. All of those dampish noses pressing
porthole glass, as the moon emerges perfect,
hanging there, like the face of someone loving
passing over the water bowl's calm surface.

THE RELEASED

(On Jessica Eaton's Quantum Pong 3, 2006,
digital c-print, 52" x 40")

The thought of losing so many of my children...
—Edvard Munch

To make that one, she said, I had my friend
climb up into the rafters, then let go
five hundred Ping-Pong balls. It was so
chaotic; this developed in the end.

You see the way they're floating? This is how
it goes when you expose sequentially:
the orbs have lost all heaviness, they're free,
like bubbles in a nothing. Listen now,

I've tried so hard to move that bloody piece
but it's so big. The smaller ones, they may
sell faster. But my Ping-Pong balls will stay
with me. Someone will cherish their release.

Anyhow, I drove it into town
to get it framed. The Chinese lady stood
for seven minutes staring. (Is that good?)
She held it up, refused to put it down,

said it was the best thing she had seen
("I only get the landscapes, but now this...").
The air filled with something like loneliness.
Her finger tracked the empty space between

as well, where ghosts waft noiselessly through light
and time. Her voice was like a violin,
all swooping phrase. She took the picture in
the back.
                    I think of Mrs Chin tonight

who left behind with aunties in Fuzhou
the greatest art conceived in happiness,
beyond the grey-scale of this world's distress.
I wonder if she's on her way home now,

Lost in a lucent universe of pearls
that ornament the dark field.
                                        Far away,
behind our dull dimension's sphere, they play,
exposed to light, three laughing little girls.

LOST TWINS

Apparently, there's nothing in the eight,
the double chamber robbed of pulse or flutter.
The grey technician's face shuts like a gate;
she switches off the patient's screen and mutters
something on the faxing of reports
(*I'm sorry, it's the obstetrician's call*).

The organism won't permit, aborts,
grows old, forgets. We're meant to see it all,
the tapestries of war, our lives' design;
each burning bolt is cheerfully explained.
The greater picture offers to refine
and, even as the warp and weft are strained,

apparently, biology is fate.
Apparently, there's nothing in the eight.

BAD INFLUENCE AND SENIOR KINDERGARTEN

I fear like blackest death the other children.
I see them streaming from the schoolyard gates.
He sees the ones he loves, and then he waits.
He's one of those whose ready heart will kill them.

They call him by his name, here in the open,
but this is an example of their arts.
I know about the sulphur in their hearts;
I know they will be rotten when they ripen.

They blink at me behind the chain-link fence.
Oh, what can stop this parliament of peers?
He'll choose them over me and join their games.

The difference that he sees will be immense;
it's written down in stone. In seven years
I have to be the person that he blames.

THE GO TRAIN ARITHMETIC SONG

Twenty-five drunks on a train.
Only one window seat free.
Thirteen dead flies on the pane.
Two hairy hands on your knee.

Seventeen soccer club mufflers
Floating in thirty-four hands.
Twenty-five vomiting shufflers
Delivered to you from the stands.

Three noses pointed your way.
Eleven mouths ask what you're reading.
Five cracks at *please go away,*
None with a hope of succeeding.

Forty-four backs in the aisles.
Seven more stops on the map.
Twenty-one wobbling smiles.
Fifty-two cans in your lap.

One and a half lousy feet
Up to the wall strip alarm.
Ten inches down to the street.
Ten fingers pried from your arm.

Fifty years flashing ahead.
What will remain of your youth?
You'll yearn for the heavenly bed;
But then, at the moment of truth,

When you have entered the dark,
There you will meet them again:
Pursuing the Stygian bark,
Twenty-five drunks on a train.

MODERN CAMERA

This is the setting for when you're inside.
This is the setting for candlelight.
This is the setting for sunrise and sunsets.
This is for portraits of people at night.

This is the setting for servings of food.
This is the setting for things under glass.
This is the setting for files and documents.
This is the setting for flowers and grass.

This is the setting for watching explosions.
This is the setting for watching the match.
This is the setting to hold to the spyhole
And see children cry when you've fastened the latch.

This is the setting for trembling hands.
This is the setting for earthquakes and fire.
This is the one for the tyrant-in-training
(You cower below them and tilt the lens higher).

This is the setting for rocks and hard places.
This is the setting for blood and ablution.
And this button here is the one that you press
When shooting yourself is the only solution.

EXPLAINING FILIAL PIETY TO MY BROTHER IN THE BAR

Agamemnon, well-intentioned dupe,
goes to bat for Menelaus. Why?
His brother's wife, a hen that flew the coop,
is lolling in the crook of Paris' arm.
Tossing curls, they go, and arrows fly,
dirty metals clash. What is the charm
of getting mired in blood relation's poop?

The boats won't go, so Agamemnon thinks
to put his only daughter on a rock,
as offering to the gods. Of course, it stinks.
Clytæmnestra has a roaring fit
and kills him in the bath (to choral shock).
So that's why I don't believe one bit
it's me who should be paying for these drinks.

A SERBIAN MAN IN A BAR SAID

This is the beast you see when you are sleeping:
a stag. A glossy shadow on the slope,
imperious and heavy, great neck curving,
poised and nervous archetype of hope.

A stag is not a doe, it is a master,
despite its feather lashes, copper gloss,
the ripple of its backbone through the birches,
and felted antlers, softer than new moss.

It was made to lord above its children;
it was made to trample for its mate,
to thrash the windscreen to a field of diamonds,
rear up on warning signs in every state.

Where and when has it known slumber?
It keeps a special covenant with sleep,
with ears that smell the guns across the marshes
and skin that hears the hunter's ageing jeep.

But those who seek the beast must see it finished;
a thing with muffled language is no good:
it charges and it tramples and it dazzles.
Its future's bound in knots upon a hood.

That is how it is now, twelve years later.
That's the beast you see when you are sleeping
in your queen bed, the highway at your ear.
The red cloud clears, then you wake up weeping.

IF I KNEW
After Matija Bećković

If I knew I could bear up with pride
In a cell, or in chains, on the stand,
I'd burn like a pyre, take it all in my stride,
Brush it off with the back of my hand.

If I knew there'd be mournful guitars
And the brute executioner's tears,
I would slip on the noose and pass out cigars,
Kick the stool out myself, with no fears.

But I fear I would crumble and plead;
I would weep on my knees and turn traitor.
If it gave me my life, I would make others bleed,
I would let myself down and pay later.

THE ENIGMA OF FATE

Last night, you left your red glove by my bed,
Eugenia. The rest of you was gone,
delivered to the other side of town,
to Heaven, and the man you wait upon.

Oh, made of marble is he, tall and blind,
Eugenia, to you, your web, your stars.
He'll never sing, he'll never read your mind;
he'll never know about this room of ours.

I love you, even gone, with one bare hand,
Eugenia. I love you when I pass
the factory gates and feel my backbone curl,
my eyes go red, my courage fog like glass.

Will someone come and sweep your chequered floor,
Eugenia? Will someone call you sweet,
put chestnuts in a basket by your door,
keep vigil when your sweat soaks through the sheet?

The syrup blue of twilight covers me,
Eugenia. A glove will not undo
the having, the not-having of a hand
in fate. The night folds in on me and you.

EULOGY FOR KEN SPADA

At thirteen, I met my first leather man;
he ran the shop a stone's throw from the hole
where I bought smokes. An ancient sable stole,
shell bangle, some weird pegged pants from Japan,

a Chinese tea dress crawling with yulan
in Vegas gold—all things picked out in droll
conspiracy for me. How he'd extol
the virtues of the A-line or a fan

I never needed, push the leopard coat
into my eager hands. A pair of eyes
like that, to youth, is dangerous and dear.

I see him now, in Charon's little boat:
he shakes his palms and, looking up, he sighs.
"These hooded robes," he says, "are so last year."

FINAL REQUEST

When I am dressed for heaven, I will wear
no wedding white, no *peau de soie* or gold
embroidery. Not me. Nor will I hold
a Bible or a snippet of your hair.
I curse the navy twin-set you prepare,
the sulky bow-neck blouse that makes me old.
If you disguise me thus when I am cold,
how will the others recognize me There?
Please put me in the muumuu that I bought
a dozen years ago. The one you hate.
The one that makes you plead with me to change
each time I put it on. I've often thought
I'd leave you in a good, embarrassed state
as I do now. So nothing would be strange.

THE HAND OF SCHEVENINGEN

The strangest thing on Scheveningen Beach,
the Netherlands' most popular resort,
is not the shining mud-sheet of the sand
that never seems to end, the glut of bars,
the walrus girls on loungers, or the roar
of grey Atlantic waters as they blow
a raspberry toward the English shore,

but rather, a perplexing ancient sign
designed to warn the swimmers of the tides:
triangular, its border painted red,
no words at all. No Hey! The Sea is Rough!
or Currents May be Strong, or Take a Boat!
No, just an image of a panicked hand
emerging from the crudely rendered waves.

It proves itself effective, as it draws
a daily crowd of tourists and the like.
They turn away from stalls of souvenirs,
from tapas bars and lurching children's rides.
They wander to the ocean's ragged edge
to gather round the pole and take it in.
It generates in each a certain fear.

There are the ones who shudder at the thought
of toddlers bumped from rowboats with an oar.
A great percentage travel back in time
to swimming tests in underheated pools.
And there are those whose minds are etched with scenes
from horror films: the reborn killer's fist
erupting from the honeymooner's lake.

I know there are, among them, even more
(the woman with the waist-encircling brute
she cannot turn her back on, or the man
who, Saturn-like in appetite, devoured
his weight in pizza when his children died,
the gambler on a quest to save the house,
the girl who can't surrender without porn)
who tilt their faces up to see the sign,
the comfort of its never-changing sea,
to see themselves in Scheveningen's Hand
and think, *Oh God, God, no, the sky, the sky.*

ACKNOWLEDGEMENTS

Earlier versions of several of these poems were published in the following literary journals: *Futurecycle Poetry, Light Quarterly, Mezzo Cammin, The Raintown Review, Softblow, Stonecoast Lines*, and *The Toronto Quarterly*. My thanks to the editors.

"Curriculum Vitae" was commissioned for performance at Signals from the DEW Line, a tribute to Marshall McLuhan, held at the Gladstone Hotel in Toronto, on November 8, 2011. The poem will be appearing in *DEW Lines, Loans and Lineages: Poetry and Poetics After Marshall McLuhan,* edited by Lance Strate and Adeena Karasick, to be published by NeoPoiesis Press.

ALEXANDRA OLIVER
was born in Vancouver, BC. Her work has
received nominations for the Pushcart Prize
and a CBC Literary Award in Poetry. The
author of one previous book, *Where the
English Housewife Shines* (Tin Press London,
UK 2007), Oliver co-edits *The Rotary Dial*, a
journal of formalist poetry based in Toronto.
She teaches in the Stonecoast M.F.A.
Program at the University of Southern Maine.